Garlic and Lavender

A Comedy

Nick Warburton

A SAMUEL FRENCH ACTING EDITION

SAMUEL FRENCH

FOUNDED 1830

SAMUELFRENCH-LONDON.CO.UK
SAMUELFRENCH.COM

CHARACTERS

The Castle
Count Drackenberg, a sinister Count
Murk, his henchman
Dolly } innocent English girls from Tunbridge Wells
Clara }
Dr Lutz, a vampire expert

Below stairs
Boris, a common servant
Trudi, common serving wench
Emmanuelle, the ghost of Count Drackenberg's previous victim

The taverns
Roger, an English gentleman
Herr Kronjarg } miserable publicans; can be played by
Herr Jargkron } the same actor
Olga } jolly barmaids; can be played by the same actor
Hilda }
Hans }
Denise } local yokels
Daisy }

The action of the play takes place in the main hall and kitchens of Castle Drackenberg and in two inns, *The Swineherd's Billet* and *The Twisted Claw*

PRODUCTION NOTE

Garlic and Lavender was written to be performed after a very short rehearsal period: its first performance came on the very day rehearsals started. However, it can also be given a more lavish production with preparations of the usual duration.

It's an ensemble piece with parts evenly distributed and acting opportunities for many. Several of the roles can be either male or female. The cast may be divided into three groups for rehearsal purposes — those in the castle itself (SCENES 1 and 4); those below stairs (SCENES 2 and 5); and those in the taverns (SCENES 3 and 6). One character from the second group bursts into the end of SCENE 6. Otherwise the final scene is the only one in which most of the cast appear together.

It's a melodrama so the acting style it demands is clear and expressive. It requires plenty of broad gestures, throbbing voices and playing out to the audience. It will be hard to go over the top, but it will work best if it's taken as seriously as possible.

It can be played with a cast of 14, but doubling can reduce this number. (Hans, Denise and Daisy could become a single character, for example.) If you have more than 14 actors to deploy, you can use different personnel for the two tavern scenes. The set, too, can vary from elaborate to basic, depending on your resources and inclinations, but it is important that the changes from scene to scene are made swiftly.

Nick Warburton

Other plays by Nick Warburton
published by Samuel French Ltd

Distracted Globe
Domby-Dom
Don't Blame It on the Boots
The Droitwich Discovery
Easy Stages
Ghost Writer
The Last Bread Pudding
The Loophole
Melons at the Parsonage
Not Bobby
Office Song
Receive This Light
Round the World with Class 6
Sour Grapes and Ashes
Zartan

GARLIC AND LAVENDER

The hall of Castle Drackenberg. A dark and stormy night

As the play begins, there is creepy music and thunder

The entrance door groans open

Dolly and Clara enter carrying small travelling bags. They are fresh, innocent creatures, given to fluttering their eye-lashes and speaking brightly

The thunder and music fade. Dolly and Clara look around in awe. During the following Clara produces a handkerchief

Dolly I say! Can this be the place, do you think?

Clara It must be, Dolly. It's the only castle we've encountered.

Dolly But there's no one here. It seems — deserted.

Clara Have you the letter still? That will tell us if we have indeed found our destination.

Dolly I have it here ... (*She takes a letter out of her bag. Reading*) "My Dear Young English Ladies, I am so glad you saw my little advertisement in *The Lady* and I am very much looking forward to entertaining you all at my snug and homely abode in Upper Kolbennblitz." Gosh, doesn't he sound polite?

Clara Indeed, he does, Dolly, but I would hardly call this snug and homely. It's large and rather too gloomy, and somewhat — creepy. And these forbidding walls — what secrets do they conceal, I wonder?

Dolly Oh, pooh, Clara. Doubtless you're upset to find it so unlike Tunbridge Wells, but that's exactly why we've come. Tunbridge Wells offers no excitement.

Clara But what kind of excitement are we to expect here? Were you not unsettled by our progress up to the castle?

Dolly Unsettled? By what?

Clara A figure in a tall hat and a large cloak, gliding behind us through the trees.

Dolly Gosh.

Clara You may well gosh, Dolly. I didn't like the cut of his jib.

Dolly Really, Clara. Is that the observation of a true St Ethel's girl?

Clara Perhaps not, but who was he?

Dolly A foreigner, without a doubt, and therefore almost certainly harmless. Do let me read on. (*Reading*) "Once you've found the village of Lower Kolbennblitz in the Cold Moon Mountains, take the winding path north to the castle. I shall await you there. Yours faithfully, Count Drackenberg."

Clara So this is the place.

Dolly A holiday with a Count. How super!

Clara But there is no Count. And I still don't like the look of it. Perhaps we should slip away now. We can put up at *The Swineherd's Billet* in the village …

Dolly Oh, don't be so sensitive, Clara. Lurking foreigners and suspicious walls, indeed. I have no intention of retracing my steps in the storm that is even now brewing outside. Besides, what could possibly happen to us here?

Clara I don't know. I just have — an uncomfortable feeling. And, after all, no one knows our exact destination. If only we'd let Roger know …

The Count appears behind them with Murk close behind him

Dolly Roger, Roger, Roger. That's all you think of. Can't you forget him for just a moment?

Count (*deeply*) Welcome to Castle Drackenberg, ladies.

The girls give a little jump. Clara drops her handkerchief

Dolly Oh! My word. You startled us.

Count Forgive me. Silent movement has become something of a habit with me. But you must be fatigued after your journey. Perhaps you will permit Murk to show you to your rooms? Murk! Take these bags to the East Wing.

Murk Of course, Master.

Murk takes Dolly by the arm

Count The cases, Murk! You will not, I hope, force me to reprimand you before our guests.

Murk Pardon me, Master. I have, as you know, been working tirelessly all night and am not at my best ...

Count You are to say nothing of your — work, Murk! Do you understand?

Murk Of course, Master.

Count Then take the cases.

Murk struggles off with the bags

The others watch him go

Dolly Do you have no other servants, Count Drackenberg?

Count But of course, my dear. Below stairs. They are mostly peasant wenches and yokels and, as such, best kept out of the way. I hope you will not be disturbed by sighting them during your stay.

Clara Count Drackenberg, should we wish to send a postcard ——

Count (*suspiciously*) A postcard?

Clara Yes. To inform our people of our safe arrival ...

Count Of course. Write your card, my dear, and give it to me. I will see that it gets to its — correct destination. Now, follow Murk and I will see you in due course. We dine at nine. (*He bows*)

Dolly and Clara exit

The Count stands still for a moment, then laughs dangerously and sweeps out

There is a pause

Dr Lutz creeps on. He wears a tall hat and a large cloak and carries a doctor's bag. He spots the handkerchief, recoils and then picks it up cautiously

Lutz (*sniffing*) Lavender! Ye gods, it's as I feared. The fiend has already lured to his foul den the two unsuspecting maidens I espied as I glided through the trees. Night after sleepless night I have spent working on the means to end his reign of terror. Those means I have safely in my bag. (*He taps his bag*) I have sped relentlessly through valley and mountain pass to get here in time. Surely I am not too late! (*He sits*) My weary body screams out to me, "Rest, Lutz! You must rest after your travails!" But my heart and conscience deny me. "You cannot rest," they say, "until you have warned them." (*He nods off for a second, and then leaps up*) No! Take hold of yourself, Lutz! By all the powers of light and decency, let them resist his devilish charms till I can speak to them — or (*tapping his bag*) bring about his downfall!

Lutz sweeps out

Music

SCENE 2

The castle kitchen, below stairs

Trudi sits at a table preparing food

Thunder. The music fades

Boris enters and stands dramatically in the doorway

Trudi Boris! What means this agitation in thy countenance?
Boris We'm be having guests.

Trudi gasps

I seed 'em comin' up the drive.

Trudi Be they — gentlemen?

Boris No.

Trudi Be they — elderly ladies?

Boris No. They be — innocent young maidens, as you do surely know they be.

Trudi Ah!

Boris (*striding into the room*) 'Tis the time of storms and great unsettlement in the air, my wench. The Count do be always havin' — guests at such times.

Trudi He will not be a-thwarted, Boris, that I knows. And he will brook no obstacle to his cravin'. We'm be in for a hard time of it if he be a-thwarted.

Boris What's to a-thwart him, Trudi?

Trudi Him that a-thwarted things the last time, Boris. Dr Lutz! Yes, Dr Lutz! The famous vampire expert!

Boris But, surely, Trudi, after their last encounter the Count did seal Lutz in a lead coffin and float him on a crude raft over the Drackenberg Falls from which no soul ever escaped with his life?

Trudi That he did. And how it be I know not, but Lutz survived, emergin' from the coffin to swear his dark revenge.

Boris Then it do behove us to balk the meddlin' doctor. For the sake of our peasant skins. Keep a look out for that doctor, my wench, or we shall not rest easy in our beds this storm season.

Trudi But, Boris, 'tis more than the meddlin' doctor we must be wary of.

Boris Why, what can thou be'm intendin' with such talk? Balk Lutz and our work is well done and sufficient.

Trudi No, Boris, 'tis not so. When I was sweepin' out the Twistin' Corridor in the East Wing, I do be hearin' a moanin' and a sighin'.

Boris A moanin' and a sighin'? 'Twas but the first winds of the storm season.

Trudi Would that it werst. But thou do ken as well as I that it betokens more and worse than storms. Besides, I do be seein' the swish of a white, white gown at the farthermost end of the Twistin' Corridor ...

Boris No! Emmanuelle!

Trudi Ah, indeed. I do fear 'twas 'er.

Boris Emmanuelle, the Count's last victim. So she be back from the dead land!

Trudi Oh, what be we'm to do now, Boris? I seed 'er aforetimes. The white, white gown and the pale, pale flesh — and the two cherry marks on 'er neck!

Boris Calm thyself, Trudi! 'Tis only an insubstantial thing she be. She intends no wickedness to the likes of we.

Trudi But should the English maidens catch sight of her, they'm sure to be afeared to their marrow and take flight and Count Drackenberg will vent his terrible wrath on us.

Boris No! That cannot be! 'Tis our duty to a-thwart the a-thwarters! Lutz and Emmanuelle both! Thou must look out for the meddlin' doctor and sound the warnin' at the first sightin' of him. He must on no account get to the Count.

Trudi And the guests, Boris? What of the guests? What must we prepare for them, Boris?

Boris Play not the innocent with me, my wench. Thou knowest well what thou must prepare.

Trudi No!

Boris Yes. The stew! Murk will come to see that it is properly done, so look to it.

Trudi And Emmanuelle?

Boris I have ways and means to deal with Emmanuelle. Come now, we must be about our business!

Boris and Trudi hurry off

There is creepy music

Emmanuelle, the French Ghost, glides on in a flowing white gown

Emmanuelle Count Drackenberg ... Count Drackenberg, I feel stirrings deep within me! Stirrings which have drawn me from my uneasy rest. Come to me, Master! Come to me alone! I will not share thee with another.

Emmanuelle glides off

The music changes and takes us into ...

SCENE 3

The Swineherd's Billet

There is a bar with two squeezy bottles (one containing garlic paste, the other mustard) on it. There is a single bar stool, empty and lit in a ghastly spotlight

When the scene begins, Kronjarg and Olga are behind the bar wiping glasses. As they speak, Olga lines up three drinks on the bar

The music fades

Olga 'Tis strange to see Kurt's stool there, so empty and unbuttocked.. I recall him always on that stool, a-supping and a-maundering.

Kronjarg Ay, and he had much to maunder about, Olga. He did odd jobs up at Castle Drackenberg, remember.

Olga Odd indeed they were, Herr Kronjarg. Worryingly odd.

Kronjarg There's precious little employment else in Lower Kolbennblitz, my maid. And Kurt would have fared well enough if only he had kept in mind the golden rule in these remote and lonely parts.

Olga What's that?

Kronjarg Never to thwart the Count. It takes a bold and reckless soul to do such a thing, a bold and reckless soul.

Olga Ay, and Kurt wert.

Kronjarg Kurt wert, indeed. He a-thwarted the Count, and he paid the price. That's why I leave his stool unbuttocked so. In memory of Kurt — and as a warning.

Olga Be not so doom-minded, Herr Kronjarg. We've had no trouble here this past year.

Kronjarg Yet when we did, what screaming in the night was heard. What blood there was. What innocent blood.

Olga 'Tis no wonder so many of the locals do their quaffing at *The Twisted Claw*.

Kronjarg A man does well to bide by warnings, that's all I'm
saying. Terrible things have befallen some folks in the shadows
of these mountains.

Olga But not to peasant folk like you and me, Herr Kronjarg.

Kronjarg No, to fair maidens of foreign complexion.

Olga And there be none such here.

*The door bursts open and Hans, Denise and Daisy come in. They
are wild-eyed and wet from the storm. They stand dramatically in
the doorway*

Olga Hans! Denise! Daisy! Why, friends, what means this rolling
of eyes and this bedraggledness?

Hans We have had a terrible time of it, cronies.

Denise The like of which we have not experienced before.

Daisy A terrible time.

Olga Then come thou in, all three, and relate the matter.

*Hans, Denise and Daisy move to the bar, take up their drinks and
drink*

Kronjarg Well, friends? What ails thee?

Hans We have this day been severely taxed.

Denise Such broil and turmoil we never did see.

Daisy Broil and turmoil and a sense of impending doom.

Olga But what cause, what cause?

The three stare at Olga and then ——

Hans
Denise } (*together*) A traffic jam.
Daisy

— and drink again

Kronjarg A traffic jam? In Lower Kolbennblitz? Never.

Hans 'Tis so, we tell thee!

Denise A coach came to the main street.
Daisy And there did alight …
Kronjarg What? What?
Hans
Denise } (*together*) Two well-decked out young maidens!
Daisy

The others gasp

Hans Ay. There they did alight.
Denise And straightway set off again.
Daisy Tracking their innocent way up the slopes to ——
Hans
Denise } (*together*) Castle Drackenberg.
Daisy
Olga No!
Kronjarg Foreign maids?
Hans Ay.
Denise From Tunbridge Wells.
Daisy 'Tis rumoured.

Hans, Denise and Daisy fall silent and look into their drinks

Olga I well remember that French wench who came calling on the
castle five years back.
Kronjarg Oh, ah. Emmanuelle.
Olga Ay, Emmanuelle. They do say she still stalks the mountains.
Kronjarg That she does. I know it. And thirsty for — blood.
Hans Well, I be thirsty for more ale!
Denise So fill the tankards again, Herr Kronjarg.
Daisy A body needs a drink when the storms be rumbling over the
mountains.
Kronjarg (*filling the glasses again*) Ay. And a body does well not
to be too far from the safety of his bed when they do arrive.
Olga But a song goes a long way to comfort the heart of a man at
such times.
Hans That it does, Olga, my pumpkin.

Denise So let's be singing, friends.

Daisy And keep the terrors of this benighted place at bay with a hearty song.

They all sing roughly and heartily to the tune of Ilkley Moor, *clink goblets and sway*

All (*singing*)   Where dost thou go when storms do break,
Storms do break,
In Lower Kolbennblitz on the Mount?
Where dost thou go when storms do break,
Storms do break,
Where dost thou go when storms do break,
In Kolbennblitz on Mount,
In Kolbennblitz on Mount,
In Kolbennblitz on Mount?

The song ends rousingly and they all laugh

Olga Oh, I do love a man as can harmonize.

Kronjarg 'Tis true, Olga, my fair dumpling. I've heard it said many times.

They all laugh

Kronjarg Ah, well may you quaff and laugh, my friends, but 'tis more than ill weather that afflicts these parts in seasons such as this.

They all laugh

   Roger enters

The others abruptly stop laughing and fall silent, staring at him suspiciously

Roger Is this *The Swineherd's Billet*?

No answer

I wonder if anyone can help me.

No answer

I am a traveller from England.

The others look into their drinks

I am searching for my fiancée. From Tunbridge Wells. I am told
by her Papa and Mama that she has come here with a young friend.
Has such a party been seen, do you know?

Kronjarg No. Not a sign.

Roger The thing is, I'm quite worried about them. They are
innocent, attractive girls with little experience of the ways of the
world beyond Tunbridge Wells. I fear that some bounder might
take advantage of them.

Silence. They all stare pointedly at the empty stool

So — you haven't seen them?

Kronjarg Hast thou money to spend, stranger? Or only questions
to ask?

Roger Little money, friend, but a great love in my heart and a desire
to avert disaster.

Hans Folks round here aren't minded to abide strangers.

Denise Especially poor ones.

Daisy With troubled countenances.

Roger I see. Then I'll bid you good night.

Olga You might try *The Twisted Claw*, half a league beyond the
village. Perchance they will have sighted something there.

Roger Thank you, girl. You have a kind heart.

Roger exits

The others immediately break into talk and laughter again

Roger returns

They stop

The Twisted Claw, you said?
Olga Ay.
Roger Right.

Roger exits

The others take up their goblets and leave, with more animated talk

Music

SCENE 4

The hall of Castle Drackenberg

There is a table with three chairs nearby. There are plates and spoons on the table

The music fades

Lutz creeps on, carrying his bag. He sniffs the air

Lutz Yes! It is as I thought! The scent of lavender is everywhere. I must strain every sinew to see that it does not become mingled with the scent of — blood. But what's this? (*Sniffing*) I detect another aroma ... Stew! Great heavens! The fiend is up to his old tricks already. Unless my nose deceives me, this is the stew that will render a maiden senseless, plunging her into the soporific depths of oblivion so that he can work his evil ways! I must work fast. (*He sits and opens his bag. He bends his head over it and, for a second, nods off again. Then he suddenly leaps up*) No, no! Lutz, you fool, you cannot give in to fatigue when danger looms round every corner of this foul place. (*He pulls from his bag a piece of paper, a container of garlic paste and a mirror*) Here are the instructions that will put a stop to his dread sport, once and for all.

(*Reading*) "Hold a mirror to the creature's face. Say the words —
'Yield! Yield! The garlic is peeled! Haste! Haste! Apply the
paste!' Then smear a paste of garlic on the creature's head." And
so I shall, or my name isn't Dr Franz Lutz.

There is a tinkle of laughter, off, as the girls approach

But hark! The tinkle of English laughter and the tread of dainty
feet on cold stone! I must hide! (*He hides behind a curtain*)

Dolly and Clara enter, ready for dinner

Dolly I'm so hungry I could eat a horse.
Clara I fear we might have to, Dolly. There seems to be precious
little else.
Dolly But the Count said we'd dine at nine. He must be intending
us to have a bite of some kind.
Clara I still think we should consider leaving. There's something
far too unsettling about this place. While I was attending to my
ablutions I heard the strangest sounds emanating from the
corridor ...
Dolly Indeed, so did I. I wonder ——

*The Count and Murk sweep in. Murk holds a large bowl and a
ladle*

Count Ah, ladies! I am glad to see that you are punctual. Do be
seated.

*The Count moves chairs into place for each of the girls, taking the
opportunity to inspect their necks as he does so. Dolly, Clara and
the Count sit*

Murk has prepared a fine stew which, I am sure, you will find —
to your taste. The stew, Murk!

Murk slops stew into each bowl. As he does so ...

You must be tired after such a journey. Do you not feel the blanket of sleep about to enfold you, my dears?

Dolly Not at all, Count Drackenberg. This is all such an adventure that I feel quite — perky.

Murk Then you'd better — eat your stew.

Clara Hmm. It smells good, Count. Do I detect carrots?

Murk Yes.

Dolly And rosemary?

Murk No! (*Shiftily*) She returned safely to her own abode. I swear it.

Dolly I mean herbs.

Murk Oh. Yes.

Clara And, unless I'm much mistaken, I think I scent the essence of — garlic.

Count Garlic! (*He stands, rigid and shaking, rolling his eyes*)

Murk No, no. No garlic.

Clara No, no. I'm sure I was mistaken.

Murk She was mistaken, Master. Calm yourself and be seated.

The Count calms himself and sits

Count Forgive me. I have a childhood aversion to … to …

Dolly Garlic?

The Count stands abruptly and rolls his eyes

To certain herbs, I mean?

Count Yes, to certain herbs. But it is nothing. It need not concern you.

Murk Now, fair maidens, delay no longer. Enjoy your stew.

Clara (*inspecting the stew*) I … I had a cream cracker earlier, I fear, and am quite bloated.

Dolly Well, I'm famished. (*She eats*) Oh, this is surprisingly toothsome, Clara. You really ought to give it a try … (*She eats another spoonful and falls into an instant swoon. She snores*)

Behind the curtain Lutz also starts snoring

Clara Dolly! What's become of her?
Count Do not disturb yourselves, young lady. A passing swoon,
that's all. I will just loosen the button at her — neck.

The Count loosens Dolly's collar and moves in to bite her neck

*Lutz, fast asleep, falls from behind the curtain. Clara screams and
Lutz wakes up and jumps to his feet*

Clara 'Tis the foreign lurker! Oh, preserve us!
Lutz Hold!
Count Lutz!

The Count sweeps round the stage, snarling

Lutz Foul fiend! Unhand that innocent creature!
Count (*advancing on Lutz*) I thought I had done for you, Lutz.
Lutz It takes more than a lead coffin and a dangerous waterfall to
stop a Lutz. Unhand her, I say!
Count But of course, my dear doctor. She need fear nothing from
me — until I've dealt with you.
Lutz (*backing away*) You cannot harm me, heartless monster! (*He
produces the garlic paste*) I have here a paste of — garlic!
Count (*recoiling*) Garlic!
Lutz (*advancing on the Count*) Yes, garlic!
Count (*backing away*) You interfering swine! Let me be about my
rightful business!
Lutz Sucking blood from a girl's neck is no-one's rightful business!
Prepare to face destruction, Drackenberg! (*He steps forward with
the paste*)

*During the following, Clara takes the opportunity to drag Dolly
off*

*Murk creeps up behind Lutz and lays him out with the ladle. He then
stamps on the garlic paste, jumps on Lutz and spoons stew into him*

Murk Eat stew, thou meddling medic!

Lutz gasps and writhes, then slumps dramatically

Count Well done, Murk! You will be well rewarded for this. Get
the peasants to deal with the body. Tell them to — dispose of it.
I shall seek out the maidens and claim what must be mine! (*He
sweeps towards the exit used by the girls but is stopped by the mess
of garlic*) And get a cloth for this.
Murk At once, Master.

The Count sweeps off and Murk hobbles off in the opposite direction

Music takes us into …

SCENE 5

The same, a little later

Lutz's body is still on stage

The music fades

Emmanuelle is heard moaning, off

Boris enters in a state of agitation

Boris A-thwarted yet again! I encountered the French wench in the
Twistin' Corridor. A moanin' and a sighin' she was. I stood fast
and defied her but she'm be cold to all entreaties. She did pass
straight through me and the chill did enter my very marrow. And
worse than this — she'm be sore aggravated now and do seek me
out — for vengeance! But hark! 'Tis her! I must be a-hidin'
myself! (*He nips behind the table*)

Emmanuelle glides on

Emmanuelle Foolish peasant! None of your class can ever stop me.
(*She laughs weirdly*) No, there is but one way to stop me and I
dread to speak of it. I dread even to think of it. The touch of pure
silver against my ghostly flesh. (*She shudders*) I shudder at the

very mention. But a low-born oaf like him cannot know this. I am safe, safe to destroy all who stand in my path!

She glides off

Boris (*emerging*) So this be the one thing to balk her now. The touch of silver applied to her insubstantial flesh! And now I bethinks me, the Master do keep silver in this very castle. Of course! Where'm be they precious silver spoons? (*He moves to dash off to search the kitchens*)

Trudi enters

Ah, Trudi. Thou art charged with disposin' of this here body.

Trudi glances at it. This is standard work for a wench at Castle Drackenberg

And be fast about it or the Master will bear down on us all with a terrible umbrage. All our doin's must be charged with great urgency, wench.
Trudi And what great doin's have put thee in such haste, Boris?
Boris Doin's of ultimate import, Trudi. I must find a spoon!

Boris exits

Trudi Of course. (*She kneels by Lutz, searches him and finds his piece of paper in his coat pocket*) But what be this?'Tis a paper. (*Reading*) "Hold a mirror to the creature's face. Say the words — 'Yield! Yield! The garlic is peeled! Haste! Haste! Apply the paste!' Then smear a paste of garlic on the creature's head." This be the means to destroy the Master! I must take it to him and happen he will not afflict us but be glad of our faithful doin's. But wait! Ponder afresh, Trudi. Here in my hands be the power to a-thwart him for eternity. I can destroy him myself and so ease our pitiful existence. But tarry awhile, there is no garlic paste! The master will have none of that dread plant in the castle. Then I to

the village must hie myself. To *The Twisted Claw* where it be
common knowledge they do keep such stuff.

Trudi drags Lutz off

Boris dashes back on with a spoon

Boris At last! A precious silver spoon! Now shall Emmanuelle be
both balked and a-thwarted to the utmost! Praise be!

Emmanuelle glides on

Boris recoils

Emmanuelle Where art thou, peasant gruff? Darest stand in my
way? I shalt melt thy bones for this and then destroy my rivals for
the Count's love!
Boris Never! Glide where thou wouldst, fair frightful fairy! I have
a spoon!
Emmanuelle A spoon! (*She gives a mocking laugh*) What do you
take me for? I scorn your spoon. I am not a spirit to be daunted by
cutlery! (*She laughs again and glides towards Boris*)
Boris (*brandishing the spoon*) Keep back, or be balked and blighted
to desolation!

Emmanuelle continues moving forward, still laughing

What's this? No recoilin'? (*He looks at the spoon*) Arrgh! The
hallmark! The hallmark! 'Tis but plated silver! I am doomed!
Doomed!
Emmanuelle Doomed! Doomed!

*Emmanuelle lifts her cloak and engulfs Boris. He screams, writhes
and dies*

And others, too, shall meet thy fate! I know where thou art, fair
maids of Tunbridge Wells. I am coming! Coming! Coming!

Emmanuelle glides off

Music

SCENE 6

The Twisted Claw. *It looks like* The Swineherd's Billet. *In fact, it could be one of those "spot-the-difference" pictures. One obvious difference is that the tavern signs are not the same. Others might be that the whole thing has been reversed — it's a kind of mirror-image. Or that the landlord has his eye-patch over the other eye, the barmaid wears a head-scarf of a different colour and so on. There is a bar with two squeezy bottles (garlic paste and mustard) on it. At the bar is one empty stool*

When the scene begins, Jargkron and Hilda are behind the bar; Hans, Denise and Daisy are their customers; they already have drinks

The music fades and the scene comes to life with a burst of laughter. Jargkron is serving Hans, Denise and Daisy with bar snacks

Jargkron Wilt have garlic paste with that, my crony? Or good, plain coarse-grained mustard? We have the both, as thou dost know.

Hans Mustard for me, Herr Jargkron.

Denise And me.

Daisy And me.

Jargkron squirts mustard on the snack

Hans 'Tis strange to see Kurt's stool.

Denise So empty and unbuttocked.

Daisy Kurt did be'm always there.

Hans ⎫
Denise ⎬ (*together*) A-supping and a-maundering.
Daisy ⎭

Jargkron Thou'd be a-maundering if thou wert Kurt. Thou knows it well, all three, why we do keep Kurt's stool so empty.
Hilda Ay. Kurt did a-thwart the Count and paid the price.
Jargkron A terrible price and great mishap and hurt.
Hilda And all that dare to thwart the Count will pay that same price and suffer Kurt's hurt when there's a thirst for blood at Castle Drackenberg.
Hans Well, I be thirsty for more ale!
Denise So fill the tankards again, Herr Kronjarg .
Daisy A body needs a drink when the storms be rumbling over the mountains.
Jargkron (*refilling the glasses*) Ay. And a body does well not to be too far from the safety of his bed when they do arrive.
Hilda But a song goes a long way to comfort the heart of a man at such times.
Hans That it does, Hilda, my pumpkin.
Denise So let's be singing, friends.
Daisy And keep the terrors of this benighted place at bay with a hearty song.

They all sing again — the same song. The song ends rousingly and they all laugh

Hilda Oh, I do love a man as can harmonize.
Hans 'Tis true, Hilda, my fair dumpling. I've heard it said many times.

They all laugh

Jargkron Ah, well may you quaff and laugh, my friends, but 'tis more than ill weather that afflicts these parts in seasons such as this.
Hilda Be not so doom-minded, Herr Jargkron. We've had no trouble here this past year.
Hans Ay! We can't be a-dwelling on such things!
Denise Such broil and turmoil.
Daisy Will no one lighten this dread mood with a cheerful word?

Hilda Ay! That shall I, my crony! Think not on disasters for tomorrow night is Quiz Night!

They all laugh, much relieved

Roger enters

They all abruptly stop laughing and fall silent, staring at Roger suspiciously

Roger Is this *The Twisted Claw*?

No answer

I wonder if anyone can help me.

No answer

I am a traveller from England.

No answer

I am searching for my fiancée. From Tunbridge Wells. I am told by her Papa and Mama that she has come here with a young friend. Has such a party been seen, do you know?

Jargkron Hast thou money to spend, stranger? Or only questions to ask?

Roger Little money, friend, but a great love in my heart and a desire to avert disaster.

Hans Folks round here aren't minded to abide strangers.

Denise Especially poor ones.

Daisy With troubled countenances.

Roger I see. Then I'll bid you good night.

Hilda You might try *The Swineherd's Billet*, half a league back towards the village. Perchance they will have sighted something there.

Roger Thank you, girl. You have a kind heart.

Roger leaves

The others break into talk and laughter again

Roger returns

They stop

I've already been there.

Jargkron But, stranger, you'm can't be a-hoping for assistance without you be parting with good gold coin.

Roger But ...

Jargkron 'Tis true. Those you speak of have been sighted ...

Roger They have? Then why didn't you jolly well say so?

Hilda For fear, handsome stranger. The two maids be seen within this yesterweek, stepping dainty up to Castle Drackenberg. But no man sets foot in the shadow of that place for fear of his peasant skin.

Jargkron For fear of doom! Doom! Everlasting doom!

Roger I see.

Hans And a man would need the backing of good solid silver.

Denise And gold a-plenty.

Daisy To face up to such a thing as that.

All Doom! Doom!

Roger (*producing a silver spoon*) I do have the silver spoon that I was born with, I suppose.

Hilda 'Tis a start, mayhap.

Roger And a little money. A pittance by the standards of Tunbridge Wells, but perchance simple-minded peasants like yourselves will find it more than ample.

Jargkron How much?

Roger Forty gold crowns.

They all gasp with wonder

Jargkron 'Tis sufficient and no mistakin'.

Roger Then — you will come with me to this place you speak of?

Jargkron No.

Hans Even for a share of such largess ——

Denise — a man would bethink himself a dozen times ——

Daisy — before treading in the shadow of ...

Hans
Denise } *(together)* Castle Drackenberg.
Daisy

Jargkron And we must bring to mind *(pointing at the empty stool)* absent friends.

Roger Who?

Hilda Kurt that wert.

Roger But there's no-one there.

Hans
Denise } *(together)* Exactly!
Daisy

Kronjarg Unless thou hast about thy person, by some slim chance, the wherewithal to foil a blood-sucking fiend.

Hilda Some paper, be it might, penned with instructions that do show a man how to trounce a brute such as the Count and still return in safety.

Roger I'm afraid not.

Hilda Then, well-fashioned stranger, 'tis little and small can be done for thee.

Roger But by all that's wholesome, will no man risk coming with me? For the sake of a sweet young girl who needs his help will no man take his pride in his own hands and venture forth?

They all stare meaningfully at the stool

Then I shall go alone. And if I go to my destruction, I shall know that I have done all I can and answered the call of pure love in my heart.

Hans
Denise } *(together)* Stranger!
Daisy

Roger Yes?

Hans 'Tis blowing a fearful forlorn storm.

Denise Thou wouldst do well ——
Daisy — to wrap up warm.

Roger heads for the exit

   Trudi bursts in

Trudi I have it here! I have the paper that will foil the blood-suckin'
   fiend, Count Drackenberg!

Everyone gasps and stares at Trudi in a tableau of frozen surprise

Music

SCENE 7

The hall of Castle Drackenberg

The music fades

*The girls run on, pursued by the Count. They stand tensed, facing
each other*

Dolly Desist, sir! No mention was made of such goings-on in your
   advertisement in *The Lady*!
Count Then feel free to complain to the editor.
Clara What is it you want with us, you bounder?

The Count laughs horribly

   Murk appears silently behind the girls

Dolly Take not a step nearer!

The Count steps nearer

Clara Remember we are English girls, sir, with English blood in
   our veins!

The Count laughs again

You will not catch us. We are two to your one, and nimble of foot from hours on the hockey field of St Ethel's! Run, Dolly!

Clara turns and runs straight into Murk, who grabs her by the arm. Dolly remains quite still

Clara Bother!
Murk Nice fleshy arms, Master. And a pleasant bloom to the cheeks.
Clara Dolly! Help!

Dolly wobbles and then swoons

Oh, Dolly! Not again! Curse that stew!
Count Poor girl. Clearly she needs — reviving.

The Count swoops on Dolly and moves to bite her neck

Emmanuelle glides on and screeches

Count (*looking up at Emmanuelle*) Emmanuelle! What are you …
Emmanuelle Master! I have come! I have returned!
Count Not now, Emmanuelle! Can't you see I'm busy!?
Emmanuelle (*swooping towards him*) Pay heed to me first, Master, and I will help you destroy them all!
Count Murk! Hold the baggage at bay!

Murk stands in Emmanuelle's path, arms outstretched. She laughs and engulfs him

As soon as Murk is down, Roger, Hans, Denise, Daisy, Trudi and Hilda burst in. Hans has a small mirror, Denise has the paper and Daisy has one of the squeezy bottles. Roger is still holding his spoon. At the moment of crisis he finds he can demonstrate considerable sang-froid

Roger Stay where you are, all of you!
Clara Roger!
Roger Unhand that maiden, you foreign cad!
Count Never!
Roger Then I shall be obliged to give you a taste of British fisticuffs.
Clara The fangs, Roger! The fangs!
Roger Don't mention it, Clara, my sweet. (*To Emmanuelle*) Here, hold this a moment.

Roger hands Emmanuelle the spoon

Emmanuelle (*screaming and staggering*) The spoon! The spoon! (*She faints away*)
Roger I say! This may prove easier than I imagined! (*He steps over Emmanuelle*) Now, sir, I am an Englishman and so I play by the book. I offer you a choice: prepare to submit to my wishes, or take a blow to the nose!
Count Never!
Roger Never what?
Count The Drackenbergs are capable of many things, English fop. Submission is not one of them.
Roger I see. (*He advances*) In that case ...
Hans (*stepping forward*) Delay, delay, young sir.
Denise A blow to the nose is as the first drop of the spring rains to such as he!
Roger What?
Daisy He don't feel it.
Hilda Use the paper, young sir!
Trudi Use the paper!
Roger Right.

Roger snatches the paper and advances on the Count. Clara pins back the Count's arms and he snarls at her

Hilda No, fine-fashioned youth! Read the paper!
Roger Oh. (*Reading*) "Hold a mirror to the creature's face. Say the words — 'Yield! Yield! The garlic is peeled! Haste! Haste! Apply

the paste!' Then smear a paste of garlic on the creature's head."

Hans holds the mirror to the Count and he recoils in horror

Count Argh!
Roger I don't blame you, sir. It's not a pretty sight. Now, wench, the garlic!

The Count struggles and rolls his eyes but Daisy squeezes the bottle at him and Roger rubs the paste in

Count ARGH!! (*He staggers about then collapses, possibly more than once*)

Everyone cheers. Clara and Roger hug

Clara Oh, Roger! You hero!
Roger It was nothing, my sweet. Anyone brought up on Wisden would have done the same.
Trudi Freed! We'm all be freed at last!

There is general rejoicing which Hilda stills with a gesture

Hilda 'Tis a great circumstance and no mistake, my cronies. And the marking of it shall be as all markings ever wert for such similar circumstances.
Trudi With a song!

They all gather themselves to sing again

Jargkron bursts in

Jargkron (*holds up his hand*) Stop!
Hilda Why, Herr Jargkron, what is it?
Jargkron 'Tis my hand, Hilda. I thought thou wouldst have know it by now.
Hilda No, no. Wherefore this halting to our well-earned merriment?

Jargkron Because we cannot abide that drear song a third time, that's why. The very sound do set my molars a-grinding and do cause my nether cheeks to clench.

The others nod and mutter agreement. They never liked the song either

Jargkron No! The proper way to mark this triumph is with a-feasting and a-dancing in *The Twisted Claw*. So back now, all of you, and tuck into a goodly basket of Jargkron's bar snacks!

Hans
Denise } (*together*) Piping hot and daubed in garlic paste withal.
Daisy

With cries of "Ay!" and "Good idea!" they all head for the exit, Roger and Kronjarg bringing up the rear

As the others leave …

Roger has a sudden thought

Roger Garlic paste, they said, my man?
Kronjarg Ay, sir. There bain't nothing like a snack bedrenched in ——
Roger But we've just used the garlic paste.
Kronjarg No, fine sir. 'Tis still lingering on the shelf yet. The coarse-grained mustard, though, be nowhere to be seen.
Roger Strange. I could have sworn …

They exit

Pause

The closing music fades up and the Lights begin to fade down, leaving a red spot on the Count

The Count stirs. He begins to rise and laugh madly as the play ends

FURNITURE AND PROPERTY LIST

SCENE 1

Off stage: Small travelling bags (**Dolly** and **Clara**)
Doctor's bag containing piece of paper, container of garlic paste, mirror (**Lutz**)

Personal: **Clara**: handkerchief

SCENE 2

On stage: Table. *On it*: food
Chair

SCENE 3

On stage: Bar with two squeezy bottles, glasses, goblets and drinks
Bar stool
Cloths for **Olga** and **Kronjarg**

SCENE 4

On stage: Table. *On it*: bowls and spoons
Three chairs

Off stage: Large bowl and ladle (**Murk**)

SCENE 5

On stage: as SCENE 4

Re-set: Paper from doctor's bag into **Lutz**'s pocket

Off stage: Spoon (**Boris**)

Scene 6

On stage: as Scene 3 but everything reversed
Bar snacks

Personal: **Roger**: spoon

Scene 7

Off stage: Small mirror (**Hans**)
Lutz's paper (**Denise**)
Squeezy bottle (**Denise**)
Spoon (**Roger**)

LIGHTING PLOT

Practical fittings required: nil
Various interior settings: a castle hall, two inns, a kitchen

SCENE 1

To open: General interior lighting

No cues

SCENE 2

To open: General interior lighting

No cues

SCENE 3

To open: General interior lighting with ghastly spotlight on bar stool

No cues

SCENE 4

To open: General interior lighting

No cues

SCENE 5

To open: General interior lighting

No cues

SCENE 6

To open: General interior lighting

No cues

SCENE 7

To open: General interior lighting

Cue 1   Closing music   (Page 28)
            Fade lights, leaving red spot on **Count**

EFFECTS PLOT